Learning for All

Lawrence W. Lezotte

Published by:

Effective Schools Products, Ltd.
2199 Jolly Road, Suite 160
Okemos, Michigan 48864
(517) 349-8841 • FAX: (517) 349-8852
http://www.effectiveschools.com

Call for quantity discounts. A version of this book is
available in videotape format.

Manufactured and printed in the United States of
America.

ISBN 1-883247-08-X

Dedicated to
Nathan and Savannah
as they begin their journey
through the system

Contents

1   A New Vision 1

2   New Ways of Thinking 5

3   Crafting a New System 11

4   Using High-Yield Strategies
to Make a Real Difference 16

5   High-Yield Strategy Number One:
Teach What You Test 20

6   High-Yield Strategy Number Two:
Opportunity Should Knock
for Everyone 26

7   High-Yield Strategy Number Three:
Time on Task = Mastery 29

8 High-Yield Strategy Number Four:
Restructure the Right Way,
Based on Research 32

9 High-Yield Strategy Number Five:
Listen to the Brain Researchers 43

10 High-Yield Strategy Number Six:
Use Technology Wisely 48

11 High-Yield Strategy Number Seven:
High-Impact Techniques for
High-Impact Learning 50

12 High-Yield Strategy Number Eight:
Create Enduring Partnerships 53

13 Building and Guiding
the Leadership Team 60

14 We Can Make it Work 66

**Correlates of Effective Schools:
The First and Second Generation 69**

1

A New Vision

Even though they can't put their finger on it, most parents and educators know that something is seriously wrong with our schools.

Some believe the problem is schools are not like they used to be when they were in school. For them, the answer is to use yesterday's school as the vision for today's school reform. Why not? For them, yesterday's schools worked!

Others believe the problem is schools are "too much" like they used to be. For them, the answer is to move further away from yesterday's schools. Why not? For them, the "good ole days" in school were simply not that good!

Actually, both views are right and wrong at the same time. The purpose of this book is to shed light on what needs to change in our schools. The book sets forth the new mission for public education and presents a set of practical steps and strategies that would, if carefully implemented, move our schools, districts, states, and nation closer to this mission.

The new mission can be stated simply—**Learning for All: Whatever it Takes!** Does it sound like an impossible dream, years away from reality? On the contrary, it is not only achievable, it is already available to us! Though accomplishing the mission will not be easy, the clear message in this book is that we can make significant progress if we are willing to take full advantage of the current knowledge base that documents and describes the processes of human learning.

If we are going to create a "new order of things" in our public schools, we must be willing to risk the criticism that will surely come. In order to advance the new mission, we will have to plan and implement change in the current system. The current system-in-place has many advocates and defenders, and they will resist change. It's a natural and very human response.

In order to advance the new mission, we will have to plan and implement change in the current system.

For those who are fainthearted, I hope you can find strength in the fact that, if we continue to do what we've been doing, we will surely continue to get what we have been getting. Is that what we want?

Right now, the aim of the current public school system is **compulsory schooling.** For many, maybe even most students, this compulsory schooling mission does translate into learning. **But this is certainly not true for all students!**

The current social/educational contract with our nation's children is as follows: "You must go to school, but once you're there, learning is optional."

In his book, *The Conflict of Education in a Democratic Society,* Robert Hutchins states the problem most eloquently, "Perhaps the greatest idea that America has given the world is the idea of education for all. The world is entitled to know whether this idea means that everybody can be educated or simply that everybody must go to school."[1]

We currently have virtually everyone going to school, so the question is, can we educate a larger and larger percentage of the population, while, at the same time, taking the whole of the population to higher and higher standards? I believe that we can and we must.

To meet this challenge, we must rewrite the social/educational contract to reflect the new aim, and then we must set out to create a new order of things. This means changing the system-in-place.

If we accept the new aim, then the implications for teachers and administrators and their work will be truly awesome. The new social contract would significantly raise the bar. The new mission states that learning is no longer optional.

We are now talking about **compulsory learning and will no longer settle for compulsory schooling.**

Attendance may be a necessary, but not sufficient, condition to assure acceptable levels of learning and performance.

I will make the following prediction. I am willing to bet that accepting the new **Learning for All** mission will be met with the same heated discussions around its desirability and feasibility as the discussions that surrounded compulsory schooling 100 years ago.

I am also prepared to predict that the first state, school district, or even individual school that has the courage to accept this as its aim, and takes the necessary steps to design a system to deliver that aim, will be the educational leader for the 21st century.

2

New Ways of Thinking

What beliefs and assumptions are necessary to support the new aim for public education?

(1) **We believe that all children can learn and come to school motivated to do so.** Let me quickly add, this belief does not imply that all children can learn at the same rate, nor do they enter the system with the same levels of readiness.

What do we say to the teacher who responds to this belief statement with the comment, "You haven't met Jimmy in my second grade class!"? It does no good to simply accuse our teacher of being wrong and, surely, we don't want to amend the belief statement to say, "With the exception of Jimmy in second grade, all students can learn and come to school motivated to do so." How do we honor the belief and the teacher at the same time?

First, we ask, "Can Jimmy walk?" If our teacher says "yes," we can conclude that he must have been motivated to learn at about age 1 to 1 1/2.

Next we ask, "Can Jimmy talk?" Again, if the answer is "yes," we can conclude that Jimmy must have been motivated to learn at about age 2 or 2 1/2.

We could go on to select other developmental tasks. Can Jimmy tie his shoes, follow commands, and so on? If the answer to each of the items is "yes," then we can conclude that Jimmy must have been motivated to learn those things that mattered to him.

What we want is for our teacher to come to this conclusion: "Jimmy is not motivated to learn what it is that I want him to learn, in the way I want him to learn it, at this time."

If that is the conclusion, our teacher is left with a whole host of reform possibilities. Maybe the teacher needs to change the

what; maybe the teacher needs to change the **when;** maybe the teacher needs to change the **how.** Once the new mission is accepted, then any and all such changes are possible.

(2) **We believe that the single school, as a system, controls enough of the variables to assure that virtually all students do learn.** The distinguished educational researcher Robert Gagne said that the essential task of the teacher is to arrange the conditions of the learner's environment, so that the process of learning will be "activated, supported, enhanced, and maintained."[2] We believe that the school can control enough of the factors to meet the conditions described by Gagne.

Any single school controls enough of the variables to assure that virtually all students do learn.

A review of the research and case literature on effective schools and effective teaching provides convincing proof that schools do have the control necessary to demonstrate the validity of this belief. Unfortunately, since learning is optional on the part of the student, assuring that all do learn is also believed to be optional on the part of too many of the faculty, staff, and administration of too many schools.

Far too few have made it their school's mission and their personal and professional passion to assure that all students do learn. Changing the mission is the first step toward making **Learning for All** nonnegotiable.

(3) We believe that the internal and external stakeholders of the individual school are the most qualified and capable people to plan and implement the changes necessary for the school to make progress toward the Learning for All mission.

The current culture of most schools projects the notion that improvement comes through new programs, new materials, or additional staff. School improvement is thought of as an add-on to the existing system or services. While I'm not opposed to these kinds of changes, they usually don't serve to advance the school toward the **Learning for All** mission.

The reason for the disappointing results comes from the fact that most new programs, materials, or staff are intended to produce more of what the system is already producing and will not change the outputs of the system significantly. Remember, the current system-in-place was never designed to successfully teach all the children. If we set out on the new mission, we will have to craft a new system.

One of the most difficult steps on the journey toward the **Learning for All** mission is getting the adults in a school to believe they can make a difference—that if they change what they do and how they do it, the results will be different.

(4) **We believe that you and your colleagues are already doing the best you know to do, given the conditions in which you find yourself.** This is an important part of the supporting belief system.

If you want to change the outputs of the system-in-place, what do you need to do? First, you have to change what people know. That is, new knowledge has to get into the system. Second, you need to change the conditions in which you find yourself. Changes in the knowledge states of the staff, without changing the conditions, or changing the conditions without changing the knowledge states, will likely yield little or no change (or worse, it could yield change without difference).

(5) **We believe that school-by-school change is the best hope for reforming the schools.** For changes at the school level to be sustained, district-level administrators and staff from agencies beyond the school district must also be committed to the new mission and dedicated to doing whatever they can to support the schools.

This represents a major change for many of the agencies because, at the moment, most central offices, state departments, regional accrediting agencies, and even some federal programs are more concerned with conformity, compliance, and control issues than with results or outcomes. If we want schools to be more dedicated to the **Learning for All** mission, as judged by student performance, we are going to have to allow processes to vary from classroom to classroom, and school to school, in order to get the desired results.

I recommend that representatives of the school-level teams and members of the central office staff form a **district-wide planning team** for the purpose of discussing district policies, practices, and patterns which serve as barriers to the **Learning for All** mission. In addition, the team could recommend policies or programs that, if implemented, would serve to sustain the changes at the school level.

The successful implementation of the ideas in this book can only be accomplished if there is a commitment to systemic change on the one hand and a commitment to extensive staff development on the other. Whatever else may be required, the lessons from successful restructuring in the private and public sectors are clear. There must be broad-based commitment to the training and retraining of the workforce.

3

Crafting a New System

In *The New Economics For Industry, Government, and Education*, W. Edward Deming defined and described a system as "a network of interdependent components that work together to try to accomplish the aim of the system."[3]

He went on to say that a system must have an aim, and a system must be managed. He noted that, in Western organizations, if the system is not managed effectively, the individual components become selfish, competitive, and independent. He also cautioned that the aim of a system must never be defined in terms of activities, methods, or programs.

Finally, he stated that, regardless of where it starts, if a system is going to be effective, a

A system must have an aim and must be managed.

pervasive sense of mission must come to characterize the organization, and this sense must extend throughout the organization. I might add that, while most schools and districts have mission statements, few can be described as having a pervasive sense of mission.

One of the most significant differences between public schools in the United States and the school systems around the world (to whom we are often compared, and found wanting by our critics) is that we have chosen to use schools as social instruments to accomplish many goals beyond learning. When I ask new building principals what part of the role requires more time than they had imagined, the most frequent answer I get is the time they must devote to the task of connecting students with needs to relevant external social services agencies.

Because of our desire to see the school as a source of social problem-solving, the schools are always on the edge of what the scholars call **goal displacement.** If we say that the values and priorities of a system can be inferred by studying how its leaders spend their time, and if we watch how most superintendents spend their time, we would conclude that schools are about the business of buildings, busses, bonds, budgets, and boards, and not about teaching and learning!

Today's schools are caught in a constant tension between competing goals, and that makes it very difficult to make sure that all the components of the system, and the individuals who work in the system, stay focused on the primary aim of the system.

At the school level, the competing missions tend to center themselves around these three basic functions:

1. Local schools are expected to serve as institutions of custodial care.

2. Local schools are supposed to sort and select students—the "talent agent" function.

3. Local schools are institutions of teaching and learning.

Don't be mislead by what I'm saying. All these different, and even competing, missions can be metaphorically on the bus to continuous school improvement. But only one of the missions can drive the bus!

What, then, is or ought to be the primary aim of the school system? I am advocating that the **Learning for All** mission be that primary aim.

Recently, a very good superintendent of a very progressive school district told me that, in his district, they have systems-in-place to manage the money down to the dime, but they don't have systems-in-place to manage the learning mission. My experience suggests that this statement is generally true of most of the 15,000-plus school districts throughout the United States today.

The journey to continuous improvement in our schools must begin with a clear declaration of the aim of the system, an aggressive strategy to insure that a pervasive sense of mission comes to characterize the entire organization, and the development and implementation of a system that makes it possible to effectively manage the mission.

With computers and other communication technologies that are currently available, there is technically no reason why school superintendents shouldn't be able to manage the **Learning for All** mission with the same level of precision that they currently manage the money.

Here is the standard we should strive to meet. If the system is doing what is needed, it should be possible for a superintendent to bring up an up-to-date student performance record on a computer screen in her office, and be able to tell the student's parents how well their child is doing, relative to the mastery of the district's intended curriculum.

If the superintendent can do this for any student at any time, she would be able to do the same thing for any aggregation of students, large or small, that would be of interest to her. For example, if we want to know how all second grade boys compared to girls, in a single school or across the entire system, are doing, it would be technically easy, once the learning system is in place.

Likewise, if the superintendent can do this, then anyone between the superintendent and the student, with a legitimate reason to do so, could also access the learning system. The school principal could monitor learning for individuals or groups of students in the school. The teacher could constantly monitor his students. The Title I coordinator or the director of the science curriculum for the district could also monitor the mission for the affected students or the affected curricular areas. The possibilities are limitless!

We have clarified the primary aim of the system, described the beliefs and assumptions that support this aim, and described the learning information system that is required to be able to effectively manage that mission. I doubt that educators will ever be able to effectively manage the schools unless, or until, they develop a system for monitoring and managing the mission.

4

Using High-Yield Strategies
to Make a Real Difference

What is meant by a high-yield strategy?

W. Edward Deming repeatedly emphasized that, in order to improve a system, you have to draw heavily upon the profound knowledge that informs the work of the system.[4] In this case, the profound knowledge includes, but is not limited to, the research on the human brain and human learning processes.

In addition, he said that we need to know how systems work, and the theories of natural variation. High-yield strategies represent those approaches to classroom and school organization and human learning which research indicates makes a predictable difference in student learning and performance.

High-yield strategies can make a predictable difference in student learning and performance.

In his book, *Knowledge for Action*, Chris Argyris distinguishes between applicable knowledge and actionable knowledge.[5] In this context, high-yield strategies represent those concepts and principles taken from research that have relatively direct and immediate application to schools, classrooms, and human learning. The staff members of the individual school will need to convert this applicable knowledge into actionable knowledge that they believe will work in their setting.

Making applicable knowledge actionable in a given context allows the leaders to take into account the history, culture, and organizational context. If you think about this statement for a minute, you'll realize why prepackaged programs rarely live up to their advance publicity. High-yield strategies are those concepts and principles that are not only research-based, but have also withstood the test of application in real-world schools and classrooms, and are found to be effective in producing desirable changes in student outcomes.

We need to introduce one more defining dimension of the concept of a high-yield strategy. Researchers have distinguished between what they call activities-driven and results-driven interventions. They used activities-driven intervention to describe activities or strategies which may be very good, but workers cannot see the cause-and-effect connections with the desired outcomes. In results-driven interventions, workers can describe the cause-and-effect linkages that form the rationale for the intervention.

In summary, a high-yield strategy is defined as a **concept or principle, supported by research or case literature, that will, when successfully applied in a real school setting, result in significant improvement in assessed student achievement.**

High-yield improvement strategies tend to be those that impact the classroom and school in such a way that they produce changes in the transactions and interactions between the teacher and students or among students.

But the opposite is also true. A great deal of time and individual and organizational energy goes into new planning systems, selecting a new superintendent, or electing a new school board. As time passes, one notices that student learning and achievement have not improved. Why? As important as such decisions may be, rarely do such changes at the top of the organization change how teachers and students relate to each other and the program of curriculum and instruction. Such changes may be worthwhile in their own right, but won't impact measured student achievement, at least in the near term.

In our efforts to train school teams to plan and implement change aimed at improving student learning and performance, **we have had our best success when we ask them to focus on two or three high-yield strategies** that will likely result in significant increases in student achievement.

5

High-Yield Strategy
Number One:
Teach What You Test

The first, and in some ways, most significant high-yield strategy is that of curriculum alignment, or teaching students what you test them on. There are four assumptions that must be considered:

(1) We start with the assumption that the school is part of a larger educational system with clear curricular goals. When asked, "What is it that this school system wants the students to

know, do, and be inclined to do when they complete their time in the system?", the school staff would be able to give very clear and precise answers.

Needless to say, if the staff can't answer the question, then that defines where the journey to school reform must begin for that school and district. Bear in mind the old expression, "If you don't know where you're going, any road will get you there!"

There is a variation on this expression that should give anyone responsible for managing the district's learning mission great pause! "If you don't know where you're going, **no** road will get you there!"

On what basis can you ask a teacher to change what he or she is doing? Remember, most people in the system-in-place like to travel on familiar roads, and familiar roads are generally seen by them as the right road. For them, it may not matter that the learning and performance do not measure up to what someone else says is the right road.

(2) We assume that the goals of education that have been specified by the respective state and local district have been translated into a coherent set of leveled and sequenced programs, courses, and instructional units.

Given a specific grade level or subject matter area, the teacher who is responsible should be able to describe the instructional content he teaches and where that content and those student learnings fit into the overall goals of the system. Likewise, the same teacher should be able to describe, with some specificity, what prior learnings the students will bring to his classroom. Mastery of these prerequisites is essential in the teacher's class or subject.

Probably the best way to meet this standard is through the process of backward-mapping the curriculum. The process suggests that we begin with the end in mind, like the architect's rendering of the finished home, and then design down. In the end, the scope and sequence should make sense to teachers, and should stand independent of the particular textbooks or other instructional materials currently in use in the school.

Every teacher should have a clear understanding of the essential student learnings for which he and his students are responsible. In this context, essential learnings are those that are deemed to be prerequisite to student success at the next levels of learning.

If any of the conditions associated with this second assumption are not met, then this represents a set of critical work activities that must be addressed by the staff and administration before the individual school can proceed much further with the remaining curriculum and instructional alignment issues.

(3) The next major step on the journey to curriculum alignment assumes that the teachers in a school can answer this question: "What evidence will the system (school, district, or state) use to judge whether the students have mastered the essential student learnings for that grade or subject?"

If teachers are able to answer this question, **we are now in a position to address the alignment between the intended curriculum and the assessed curriculum—** the one that is used to judge progress on the curricular goals and objectives. If the teachers in the school cannot answer the evidence question, the next critical work activity would be to select the assessment system that will be used. Much has been written regarding the best type of assessment system for monitoring student learning as reflected through student performance.

It is important to remember that the learning system we are developing is predicated on the belief that assessments should be curricular-based and criterion-referenced.

Curricular-based, criterion-referenced assessment is consistent with the mission of **Learning for All**.

(4) When the first three assumptions have been met, the educators can now be engaged in the process designed to meet the following standard:

As a teacher, you should come to be convinced in your head, heart, and gut, that if you teach the intended curriculum, and the students learn it, they will perform well on the assessment measures.

Few school districts can meet this standard and the result is great anxiety on the part of the organization. Two controversial ideas may help to bring the importance of these issues into focus.

First, curriculum and assessment alignment is a moral issue. If the adults don't do what needs to be done to meet the assumptions listed in this chapter, the consequences of their negligence fall most heavily on those students who are most dependent on the school as their source of academic learning— namely, the children of the poor.

Second, teachers need to be told that it is O.K. to teach students things they will not be tested on. But a teacher would have to be crazy to test children over things they haven't been taught. Said another way, if you want to look bad as a teacher, one of the surest ways to do so is to teach one thing and test the students on another.

The four assumptions set forth here are essential prerequisites to instructional alignment. Remember, our experience suggests that a school or single teacher can realize a significant "bump" in student achievement if there is tight alignment between the intended, taught, and assessed curriculum.

A school can realize a significant gain in student achievement if there is tight alignment between the intended, taught, and assessed curriculum.

The alignment of the intended and assessed curriculum sets the brackets, and the instructional delivery system must fit inside those brackets. The issue of instructional alignment rests on one of the best kept secrets in American public education: **Students do tend to learn those things they are taught.**

6

High-Yield Strategy Number Two: Opportunity Should Knock for Everyone

Over the years, teachers have developed any number of ways to manage the opportunities students have to learn and practice what it is that has been defined as essential student learnings. Sometimes, almost without notice, teachers will place students in groups, and then use the group as the basis for providing the different groups different opportunities to learn.

A typical example might be to place students in groups, and then arrange the instructional tasks in a hierarchy, so that the students are expected to proceed from A to B to C. Some of the groups that move a little slower may never get the opportunity to learn and practice certain tasks or skills. If the limited opportunities include material over which the students will be assessed, these students are at a disadvantage because they didn't have the opportunity to learn.

It is critical to differentiate between those things that students had the opportunity to learn, but didn't, from those where they never had the opportunity to learn in the first place. The **lack of opportunity** to learn is often interpreted as a **lack of ability** to learn.

As the individual states have raised the stakes associated with testing and accountability, this problem seems to be becoming even worse, especially for poor and disadvantaged students.

Intentionally or not, schools often discriminate in how they distribute opportunities to learn. Take the case of two U. S. History classes taught by two different teachers in the same high school. Do you think that it would be fair to give both classes a standardized test that covers all of U. S. History when one class only studied U. S. History up through 1900? Reasonable people would say that the students in this class were at a disadvantage since they did not have the opportunity to be taught and to learn a significant part of the material over which they would be tested. Unless you spend a lot of time in schools and classrooms, you have no idea how frequently the lack of opportunity to learn before being assessed occurs!

One final example should remove any lingering doubt about the importance of the problem of opportunity to learn. This illustrates the problem with an example currently beyond the control of the school. Children who enter kindergarten from middle class, more advantaged homes have, on average, two or more years of formal schooling prior to kindergarten (usually in the form of nursery school or preschool). Children who enter kindergarten from poor and disadvantaged homes have, on average, one year or less of formal schooling prior to kindergarten, usually in the form of day care.

The lack of opportunity to learn is often interpreted as a lack of ability to learn.

Do you believe that it is reasonable to place both groups of children in the same kindergarten class simply because they are both five years of age? The differences between these two groups of children have much less to do with ability to learn and much more to do with opportunities to learn prior to kindergarten.

28

7

High-Yield Strategy
Number Three:
Time on Task = Mastery

One of the most critical decisions every teacher must make many times every day is how to best allocate one of their most precious and finite educational resources—student time on task.

In the best of all worlds, the teacher wants to allocate the right amount of time to the right tasks for each student—neither too much nor too little. Too little time allocated would mean that learning to mastery was not reached. Too much time would mean lost time to some other equally important instructional area, and probably student boredom.

We do know that there is a strong correlation between time on task and increased student achievement. That is, more time spent on the teaching and learning of reading usually results in more students becoming better readers.

There is a strong correlation between time on task and increased student achievement.

Perhaps as important as the actual time allocated by the teacher is the teacher's willingness to monitor and adjust the allocated time on task, as indicated by feedback on student learning and student performance.

I'm afraid the issue of time and its uses will continue to be a source of tension and frustration for teachers for a long time to come. Clearly, most teachers recognize that they are expected to teach far more content than is feasible, given the limited time that is available to them. Teachers need the guidance that comes from the various curriculum alignment strategies presented in Chapter 5. The only added rule of thumb that may be offered to the teacher is that, given the mission of **Learning for All**, it is more important for students to learn the content that is covered than for the teacher to simply cover the content. If it takes more time for some students to succeed, then we must find more flexible time structures.

Academic engaged time may be defined as the amount of time the students are actually, meaningfully, and productively engaged in assigned learning tasks. Teachers may have made reasonable allocations of time, but if the nature of the tasks is such that students are not focused, then they tend to be easily distracted by any number of things that may be going on in the classroom or school.

The genius of good teachers is to develop instructional tasks and student activities that motivate the students, and hold their interest throughout the instruction. When students are asked to engage in tasks and activities that require them to be active rather than passive, for example, their academic engagement rates tend to increase.

The recent research of Herb Walberg and Lorin Anderson, looked directly at time and its uses, and what they found was somewhat discouraging. They reported that typical schools lose as much as 40 percent of their available time; only about 60 percent of the allocated time is spent with students academically on task and engaged.[6]

Clearly, school reform should take this loss into account and seek strategies that would result in schools and classrooms being more efficient in their use of the available time.

8

High-Yield Strategy
Number Four:
Restructure the Right Way,
Based on Research

It should be obvious that if schools are going to be responsible and accountable for the successful learning of all students, they are going to have to restructure the way they organize to do business.

If schools are going to begin the hard work of restructuring, then it only makes sense to base the new systems, structures, and strategies on principles and concepts of learning that have been proven to be effective by research and implemented successfully in real-world classrooms and schools.

Arguably, Professor Benjamin Bloom at the University of Chicago is perhaps the one educational researcher whose scholarly contributions have had the greatest impact on educational practices in public schools in the United States in this century. His work on the Mastery Learning Instructional Model represents one of the most powerful, yet underutilized, high-yield strategy for improving student achievement available to teachers today.[7] He demonstrated that **teachers can develop and implement approaches to group instruction that are nearly as effective as one-to-one instructional tutoring models.**

He reported significant increases in student achievement when teachers used strategies based on mastery learning precepts. If the teacher then added the step of assuring that the students had met the prerequisites for what was about to be taught, additional achievement gains were noted. Further gains were noted when teachers provided enhanced instructional cues and made sure that students had opportunities for active participation.

One school district that implemented the Mastery Learning Instructional Model reported that it realized nearly a 30 percent gain in assessed student achievement when teachers were able to take their students through one "reteaching loop." Imagine how wealthy a consultant could become if she could guarantee a private sector manufacturing company a 30 percent gain in productivity by installing one innovation!

Why do schools seem to reject this type of instructional approach? My bet is that they would enthusiastically embrace such strategies as soon as student learning is no longer optional.

There are two principles of effective instruction:

(1) Place students at an appropriate level of difficulty, so that they will be challenged and can succeed—a level neither too high nor too low. We don't tend to do this because most schools place students on the basis of chronological age. This makes no sense from a student learning point of view, and, in fact, makes the teacher's job more difficult.

As adults, most of us have had experiences where we found ourselves in learning situations where the instruction was at a level that was too difficult. A common example in today's world would be computer training.

Some adults are more advanced than others, even though the group may all be professionals. What has been your experience when you feel the lesson is beyond where you are and you don't want to be embarrassed? Many of us would give up! In school, many students give up and sometimes stop trying altogether for the same reason.

What has been your experience when you find yourself in a learning situation with other adults and your skill level is above that of the instruction? Usually, we find ourselves bored and our minds begin to wander to work on our desk, errands we have to do, and so on. You guessed it—the same thing happens for students. The main difference between bored children and bored adults is that most adults have enough self-restraint to not start talking with their neighbor (remember, I said "most adults" have the necessary self-restraint—not all!).

Let me extend the example one more time to illustrate the final point. In the computer class for adults where some are much more knowledgeable than others, would the problem be solved or even reduced by placing adults in groups based on their age? I sincerely doubt it!

(2) Keep students at that appropriate level long enough so that they will succeed—neither too long nor too short. We don't tend to do this either, because we place students in age-based groups for the entire school year.

If we go back to our example of the adult education computer class, we can quickly illustrate the problem of time on task. Obviously, our more advanced colleagues should begin the lesson at the level where they will be challenged and be given the needed time to learn the new materials and skills. Likewise, our less skilled colleagues should begin their lesson at the level that is appropriate for them, and they should be given the necessary time to learn the new content and skills. The time needed for both learners to succeed is different, and the system should be able to adapt to the different time requirements.

What would a school begin to look like if it decided to restructure itself around these two instructional principles? These principles beg for the **ungraded, continuous progress, flexibly scheduled instructional system**. Such a system would include **cross-age achievement groupings** that are **fluid and continuously being changed** to provide every student the opportunity to learn to mastery.

This is already being undertaken by some schools as they systematically reform themselves around ungraded primary units and other similar structures. My sense is that such organizational strategies constitute a major step in the right direction. The grade-bound nature of today's school is part of the problem, and not part of the solution.

While ungraded primary units are a good place to start abandoning the grade-bound nature of the school, eventually the entire system has to change. What do you do with children when they leave the ungraded primary unit? Place them in a graded fourth grade? I don't think so!

The grade-bound nature of today's school is part of the problem, and not part of the solution.

Unfortunately, this systemic reform is made more difficult by the fact that the grade-bound nature of the school has taken on social and political overtones. Parents judge the worth and status of their own children and those of others by the grade they are in relative to their age. Children who seem to be in a grade usually reserved for older children are said to be unusually bright. The reverse is also true. If a child seems to be old for his grade, he must be less bright, maybe even dull. Maybe we ought to invent a whole new set of terms, since grade levels have taken on so much additional baggage.

Such systemic changes have to be implemented very carefully and probably more slowly than would be desirable. Otherwise, the resistance from both the educators and parents would likely derail the effort. We have seen far too many attempts at systemic reform fail because they failed to create a critical mass of support among the stakeholders in or outside the school.

Many elementary and middle schools have successfully begun the journey of systemic reform toward continuous progress, flexibly scheduled models by adopting Lynn Canady's Parallel Block Scheduling Model.[8] This model restructures available time, so teachers have larger blocks of uninterrupted, instructional time with a smaller group of students. Canady's research indicates that most schools have the resources needed for the model and, once implemented, teachers like it. Most importantly, **student achievement increases**!

Other schools have found success in changing the school calendar and, in some cases, even beginning school at a younger age. Some schools, especially those that are working with concentrated populations of economically disadvantaged students, are offering preschool programs in an attempt to solve learning problems before they occur. Ultimately, that has to be a major part of the **Learning for All** mission.

Recent data from the Office of Education indicates that the vast majority of middle class children has two or more years of nursery or preschool prior to kindergarten.[9] Economically disadvantaged children, on the other hand, tend to have only one year of schooling prior to kindergarten and it is more likely to be day care.

Anyone who has taken the first course in child growth and development knows that it makes no sense to ignore the age 0 to 5 period, and then hope to compensate for any cumulated deficiencies and disadvantagements later.

One example of a change in school calendar would be the year-round school concept that has become popular in some sections of the country. A typical example is the 45/15 model where students attend school for 45 days and then have a 15-day intercession. The intercession is used by some to help provide more time to those students who need it in order to assure mastery. Some students use it to explore extracurricular activities they might not otherwise have a chance to experience in the regular school schedule.

The 45/15 model tends to significantly reduce the losses in learning that occur over the traditional three-month summer vacation. An added benefit of this model is that some of the intercession can be used for staff development and curriculum work, which we know is a scarce commodity in most school districts.

Another example of restructuring, based on the principles of effective instruction from the high school, is the block scheduling model mentioned earlier. To understand this change, we need to be reminded how most secondary schools are currently structured. Most secondary school students take a set of classes for the entire semester or school year. Each class generally meets everyday for about 50 minutes. If a student successfully completes one of these courses, s/he gets one credit toward graduation. This unit is called the Carnegie Unit. Typically, a student needs to earn some number of Carnegie Units in selected subject areas to graduate.

This process served secondary education well when we had no better system of keeping track of the learning experiences of students. **Unfortunately, the amount of time one spends in a class (sometimes referred to as seat time) tells us very little about what (if anything) they have learned.**

Many secondary schools are beginning to move away from the fixed seat time model. Often, the first step toward the elimination of this old model is to "block schedule" students. This can be done in many different ways. Basically, block scheduling restructures the schedule, so students take fewer classes per semester, but the classes meet for twice as long. While this restructuring of the short-class period model is still technically within definition of the Carnegie Unit, it does allow the teacher and students much greater flexibility in how they use the larger block of time.

As we shift to a student-performance-based, results-oriented accountability system for schools, block scheduling allows educators to change the instructional process and, ultimately, abandon the Carnegie Unit model altogether. Even the Carnegie Corporation for Teaching (the developer of the Carnegie Unit) has encouraged abandoning the Carnegie Unit and replacing it with the Carnegie Competencies. Let's hope secondary schools heed their advice. With the new order of things calling for evidence of results and student performance, the process-oriented measures will no longer be sufficient.

In England, all students are expected to meet specified performance standards in algebra. Students are permitted to take algebra as a 9-week, 18-week, or 36-week course. It's not about seat time, but about meeting the agreed-upon performance standards, and the standards don't vary by the length of the course.

Obviously, those students who find algebra easy tend to take the more concentrated course, so that they can get on with other parts of the curriculum. Likewise, those who have more difficulty tend to choose a longer course sequence. Wouldn't it be nice if we could get to this model without having a lot of negative stereotyping of students who take longer to get to the same performance standards as others?

Secondary schools that are moving toward block scheduling, creating longer blocks of say 100-minute rather than 50-minute periods, are taking steps in the right direction. Block scheduling, for the most part, still maintains the integrity of the Carnegie Unit, but does repackage it into a more sensible instructional model. However, before the journey to school reform is complete, the Carnegie Unit based on time must go.

We can't continue to cling to a process culture when we are being compelled by the new mission into a results-oriented world. **New missions call for new means!**

9

High-Yield Strategy
Number Five:
Listen to the
Brain Researchers

Developing and implementing changes in instructional strategies based on recent brain research and the cognitive sciences represent a particularly promising high-yield strategy.

Coupling modern technologies with contemporary brain research has provided a much better understanding of how human learning occurs and what needs to happen to assure retention of what we have learned. Researchers have believed for a long time that something changes in the brain when we learn something new. The availability of the neuron microscope has made it possible to observe that, when we learn something new, we actually change the structure of the brain.

This insight has led to many important principles that should be followed when dealing with human learning. For example, it is generally believed that all new learning proceeds from existing learning. We build upon what we know. This being the case, if we want learning to occur, it must be meaningful to the learner. The learner must see the connections between something they already know and what it is that they are trying to learn. Good teachers know how important it is for the learner to make those connections. That is why the teacher works so hard to make the lessons meaningful through metaphors, interesting stories, or demonstrations of how the new knowledge can be applied to real-world situations.

For learning and retention to occur, the content must be meaningful to the learner.

Professor Seymour Sarason, in *Letters To A Serious Education President*, says teachers must stop trying to bring the learner to the curriculum and start bringing the curriculum to the student.[10] Professor Sarason recognized that the learner must see the new learning in terms that make connections for him or her.

Teachers should always strive to "package" the new learning inside the interests of each student. Clearly, **this change is going to represent a major shift in the instructional paradigm for many teachers.** Managing a change of this magnitude will require teachers to know the intended curriculum and their students well enough to make these meaningful connections. The skill of making meaningful connections is called **task analysis**. Most teacher training programs either ignore or give only fleeting attention to this critical concept.

Providing **advanced organizers** for students is another of the concepts from the cognitive sciences that is both related to task analysis and tends to assure high-yield increases in student learning and performance. Advanced organizers give the learner a model, picture, or rubric of what the lesson is all about. When teachers incorporate advanced organizers, student comprehension and retention increase significantly. Obviously, the inclusion of advanced organizers can take many forms, and will vary from discipline to discipline.

One of the most important lessons to be learned and applied in the classroom from contemporary brain research is the critical importance of providing the learner with **immediate feedback**. The basic instructional model by which the individual child learns to manage his/her learning in its simplest form goes as follows: The child acts, reflects on the consequences of the action, and learns a new response. (The baby responds to a parent's command. The parent praises the response. The child finds the praise satisfying and is more likely to respond in the same way again, given the parental command.)

In the current classroom organization, the teacher has 25 to 30 students, all acting and trying to wait for feedback to learn if the action was appropriate or not. Teachers simply cannot give that many individuals the feedback they need in a timely fashion. Fortunately, technology, especially the computer, may provide part of the answer, because it can be programmed to give immediate feedback to the learner's responses.

Finally, one of the other areas of classroom instruction that can and should be modified based on the brain research is **reteaching**. In the usual sequence of teaching, the teacher plans a lesson and teaches it. Some students learn and others do not. If the system would permit it, most of the students who didn't achieve mastery could, if the teacher would simply teach the lesson a second time. Most teachers have difficulty doing the reteaching, because they aren't sure what to do with the students who did learn the lesson the first time. We can solve this problem as soon as we decide that we want successful **Learning for All.**

10

High-Yield Strategy
Number Six:
Use Technology Wisely

Technology will be essential in significantly advancing the public school's new mission of **Learning for All**.

Using computers as an integrated part of the instructional program will make it possible for teachers to individualize instruction in a way which is virtually impossible without them. In addition to providing a much richer information base at the fingertips of and under the control of the learner, computers can simultaneously simplify classroom management tasks, such as record keeping, and generally enhance the learning environment.

Computers can provide students with immediate feedback on their work, complete with hints and helping strategies to further their understanding, while simultaneously compiling and maintaining a record of the students' work. Both teachers and students are ahead.

Computers, used correctly, can significantly enhance the learning environment.

We need a general word of caution here since technology is especially vulnerable to one particular problem. **Schools need to avoid the trap of "change without difference"** when introducing any new instructional technologies into the classroom.

In a high school classroom I recently visited, the students were busy using the new computers to type in the answers to the questions at the end of the chapter of the textbook. The program was not designed to provide the students with immediate feedback on their work. Answering questions at the end of the chapter can be done using a three-cent piece of paper and a five-cent pencil; we didn't need a $3,000 computer!

11

High-Yield Strategy
Number Seven:
High-Impact Techniques for
High-Impact Learning

I know many school people still persist in the belief that learning is an individual, exclusively psychological matter, best stimulated by competition where the one winner takes all.

In fact, the research tends to suggest that learning is as much a social phenomenon as it is a psychological one. Classrooms that use appropriate and well-tested cooperative or team learning strategies are creating win-win opportunities for all students.

Learning is as much a social phenomenon as a psychological one.

Some are opposed to **cooperative learning** because they feel that the most able learners will do all the work and the less able will simply ride on their coattails. This does not happen if all the students know, from the outset, that each student is expected to demonstrate proficiency, and no one will be able to hide in the group.

Others argue that cooperative learning is not fair to the more able learners. To date, the data do not support this point of view. As a matter of fact, parents of the gifted and talented should insist that teachers use this approach because it helps these youngsters to understand the lesson at a much deeper level. If we believe the wisdom of the adage, "you never learn something as well as when you teach it," we ought to insist on cooperative learning experiences for all students.

Similarly, **cross-age tutoring** has been found to be a useful high-yield instructional strategy. If you are ever asked to name one instructional practice that has strong empirical support, but is used infrequently in school, one good answer would be cross-age tutoring. A review of the literature on tutoring is impressive, yet few school improvement plans tend to include tutoring as a high-yield strategy. Why?

In my view, a major part of the explanation can be found in the existing classroom and school structures. Cross-age tutoring models, where older children tutor younger children, add value for both the tutor and the tutee. Unfortunately, to make it work effectively, teachers in at least two grade levels have to agree to collaborate and coordinate schedules, so the students can get together.

Since most schools are poor examples of collaborative organizations, most teachers would rather stumble along, even knowing that tutoring, as a strategy, is win-win. **When we change the mission from compulsory schooling to compulsory learning, high-yield strategies like tutoring would be a part of what it takes to achieve our new mission.**

I've tried to present a list of organizational and pedagogical strategies that have a proven track record when it comes to enhancing student achievement. This list is by no means exhaustive; rather, it is intended to suggest what schools can do if all of the members are willing to dedicate themselves to the new mission and draw upon the existing knowledge base to guide the change process in their school and classroom.

12

High-Yield Strategy Number Eight: Create Enduring Partnerships

I want to add one more critical, essential strategy that will be invaluable on the journey of **Learning for All**. This strategy can be summarized under the general notion of the school as a learning community. In this section, I speak to the external stakeholders who can and should be partners in the learning community of the school.

The education of a child is much broader than the learning that takes place in the school, even under the best of conditions. If this is so, then those other educative settings and people ought to be thought of as **implicit** partners in education. I firmly believe these partnerships

The education of a child is much broader than the learning that takes place in the school.

must be made **explicit,** especially for the children of the poor.

In an earlier time, schools focused on teaching young children the skills that had to be mastered for them to become good readers. The teachers assumed that parents, as partners, would read to and with their children, answer questions raised by the reading, and generally provide a forum for both nurturing the child and practicing the skills learned in school. In most cases, this partnership was both dependable and effective.

Today, schools teach the skills, but far too many students go home and watch television. They come back to school the next day, and the school teaches more skills, followed by more television, and so on. What's different or missing in this learning system? **Practice on the home-side!**

If this is an accurate picture of what is happening for more and more of today's children, then the school has to do one of three things in order to significantly improve reading achievement:

1. The school needs to get state accountability systems to assess how much kids have learned from the television programs they routinely watch! (Remember, children tend to learn best what they do most.) Obviously, this is not a sensible solution.

2. Educators could try to reestablish the old system and renew the old partnership. This is a possible solution for some, but would not positively impact a large and growing number of children for whom there is little or no home support system.

3. The school could restructure itself, so that it can both teach the skills and assure the settings at school for the missing element of individually guided practice. Either the school is going to have to abandon something else that is part of the day and reallocate the time to this guided reading practice or it is going to have to lengthen the school day.

These reform strategies are both feasible and desirable. However, they require significant and sustained commitment by all staff to the **Learning for All** mission.

It seems that many strategic planning efforts by schools and districts focus on the wrong target. They tend to focus on what can be done to improve the school and schooling, and thus fail to see the power of the partnership. If we set our sights on **Learning for All**, then the implicit partners in the educational process of children become an important resource since these partnerships are part of what it will take to achieve the mission.

Partnerships between school and home are just a start. **Other nonparent members of the community can play a very valuable role in the Learning for All mission**. For example, grandparents, senior citizens, and volunteer groups can provide additional help and powerful role models for young students. Many senior citizens feel left out, bored, and without a sense of purpose. Finding ways to involve them in the school on a regular basis not only gives the teachers the help they need and provides valuable support to students, but gives seniors a chance to contribute and make an important difference in the life of a child.

School-business partnerships are increasing in popularity and serve to bring business men and women into schools and classrooms on a regular basis. Actually, business partners often tell me the schools do not ask enough of them. I would like to be so bold as to suggest that the school should never ask for money—that's too easy for the business. Instead, the school should focus on asking for commitments of time and energy that will have a lasting payoff.

I would like to suggest that **every school principal join a local service club** (the Rotary Club, Kiwanis, etc.) and, whenever the group meets, the principal should take a teacher as a guest to the meeting. It would be even better if the teacher could also be an active member, but this is sometimes difficult if the meetings tend to occur during the school day.

My logic for encouraging this is to reconnect the school and classroom with the larger community. Most adults, especially those without children or without school-age children, are getting their information about today's schools from secondhand, or even thirdhand, sources and, thus, they are often getting very distorted images of their own local schools and teachers.

I would also like to suggest that, if possible, at least once or twice during the school year, the service club actually meet and eat at the school. We need to have a variety of strategies for assuring that members of the larger community get an up-close-and-personal look at their schools.

One additional strategy is probably most appropriate for high schools. I would like to encourage high schools to **recruit adults from the community to take classes during the school day,** right alongside the students. Small business owners in the community may gladly release their workers and pay tuition for them to take computer courses during the school day. If one percent of the students in a high school during the regular school day were adults on assignment from their place of work, the school climate would change dramatically. Teachers would quickly come to realize that these nontraditional learners are allies in setting and maintaining a positive, safe, and orderly learning climate.

Another approach to creating seamlessness between the school and the community is to have **significant learning activities actually occurring in the community.** This not only validates what the school is teaching, but gives the students an opportunity to experience those critical workplace skills that so many of our critics say are missing in our children's education today.

This strategy may be most logical for high school students and businesses in the community, but ought not be limited to these students. I feel that all students can benefit from such community-based learning projects. Every community has some unique ways to get the students to touch their own futures and educators should capitalize on them.

One partnership strategy that is receiving a lot of recognition from teachers at all levels of schooling is the **student-led parent/teacher conference.** This strategy of parent conferences is especially appropriate when the school begins to move toward more authentic assessments and portfolios for monitoring student learning and student achievement. It provides an excellent model for teaching students presentation skills, goal setting, personal responsibility, and accountability. I would encourage all school teams to at least explore this strategy. I would argue that supporters of the current approach to parent conferences would be pressed to prove that it adds value to the school's learning mission, especially when you think of how much it costs in both time and dollars.

The school as a learning community represents an important way schools can advance the **Learning for All** mission. There is a large and growing body of research and proven practices around the learning community concept, and educators should study that literature as they consider how they can best create a new order of things.

13

Building and Guiding the Leadership Team

In many ways, it would probably be easier to build an effective **Learning for All** system from scratch, since we would not have to contend with the system that is already in place. Unfortunately, this is not going to be possible and we have to find ways to transform the system-in-place into the **Learning for All** system.

Most people agree that effective strategies for initiating and sustaining human change are the weakest link in the knowledge base in the school reform discussion. While the knowledge base is thin, some basic guiding principles would, if used appropriately, increase the odds in favor of sustained school change.

Let us start with one of the core beliefs of this model for school development: We believe that teachers and administrators are already doing the best they know to do given the conditions in which they find themselves. If this belief is true, then school change is going to require two things. First, new knowledge is going to have to make its way into the system. Second, the conditions are going to have to change to accommodate the new knowledge. For best results, we need to do both in a coordinated way.

The concept of bringing new knowledge and skills to the people in the school will take the form of **staff development.** The concept of changing the conditions will be guided by a leadership group such as the **school improvement team**. It will require the cooperation and commitment of all of the teachers and administrators in the school. Therefore, the best way to build this broad-based commitment to the goals and strategies is through involvement of the staff and administrators.

Achieving the new mission will require the cooperation and commitment of all of the teachers and administrators in the school.

In addition to the involvement itself, staff commitment and sustaining school reform can be enhanced if the leadership group is guided by the following general rules:

1. It is better to have a few well-researched and well-developed goals—two or three—than it is to have many goals where the energy for change gets sprayed across the school.

2. When the leadership team sets the improvement goals and develops the action plans for their implementation, they should be sure that each goal and strategy addresses training and technical assistance, models of success, and networks of support.

Training and Technical Assistance

The school leadership team, regardless of the particular high-yield strategy selected, must consider the following question: "What training and technical assistance will be made available to whom and when?" It is unlikely that school improvement efforts will be successful without carefully planned, quality training and technical assistance.

To the extent possible, technical assistance should be made available to individual teachers on an "as needed" basis. Some teachers will need both individual advice and encouragement if they are going to be successful in implementing change.

Providing Models of Success

The school leadership team should consider what models of success it can bring into the school to provide good illustrations of the kinds of changes called for in the improvement goal. This step is not intended to have the school staff simply copy someone else's goals and strategies. Rather, it represents an attempt to provide those who have to do the changing with some approximations of what the change looks like when done well. My experience suggests that rubrics or models of good practice help to lower the levels of resistance that are likely to exist for some staff.

Models of success can come in many forms—written materials, video materials, or presentations by consultants or expert teachers. Models can also be found by having staff visit other schools where similar practices have been successfully implemented.

Networks of Support

Generally speaking, schools as workplaces are poor examples of collaborating organizations. Research suggests that, if a teacher encounters difficulty in managing the changes called for in the improvement plan, the most likely response is for the teacher to retreat further into isolation. Teachers think something is wrong with them and no one else is having difficulty.

The school leadership team needs to establish a network of support for all staff, relative to the innovation. This network ought to represent a safe and trusting setting where teachers would be encouraged to talk about the good, the bad, and the ugly of the innovation. When such networks are created, and when teachers are willing to discuss their problems, several good outcomes are likely:

1. The teacher is likely to learn that she is not alone and that, in itself, is reassuring.

2. Some of her colleagues may be able to provide advice, based on their own experience with the innovation.

3. If teachers provide feedback on what is and is not working, the school leadership team will learn about the systemic problems that were created when the change was introduced in the school and classroom system.

Any change in a system is likely to cause both intended and unintended consequences. Similarly, some of the changes will likely be positive and some may well be negative.

Monitoring and documenting the steps and stages in the implementation of an innovation in a system is very useful, but rarely done. When our strategy works, we need to be able to anticipate questions like, "What did you do first, second?" or

"If you had it to do over again, knowing what you know now, what would you do differently?"

The leadership group needs regular and useful feedback at every step throughout the implementation process.

14

We Can Make it Work

Throughout this book, I have suggested a number of high-yield strategies that would move schools toward the new aim of **Learning for All**. I have suggested how the leadership team responsible for planning and implementing change can increase its chances for success by using the current knowledge base of effective staff development, effective teaching, and planned change.

Many years ago, Ron Edmonds, one of the noted pioneers in the Effective Schools Movement, said, "We can, whenever and wherever we choose, successfully teach all students whose schooling is of interest to us. We already know more than we need in order to do that. Whether we do it or not will finally come to depend on how we feel about the fact that we haven't done it so far."[11]

It is time for compulsory schooling to be transformed into compulsory learning.

I believe the time has come to take what we know and make a renewed commitment to the American dream. It is time for compulsory schooling to be transformed into compulsory learning. We now know what it takes.

It's time to turn that knowledge into action.

Correlates of Effective Schools:

The First and Second Generation

A number of schools have been relying on effective schools research as the framework for their school improvement program. After three or four years, many claim that they have successfully met the criteria described in the research on the correlates of effective schools. These educators ask if there is anything that comes after, or goes beyond, these standards.

The concept of second generation correlates attempts to incorporate the recent research and school improvement findings and offers an even more challenging developmental stage to which schools committed to the **Learning for All** mission ought to aspire.

There are two underlying assumptions to keep in mind: First, **school improvement is an endless journey.** Second, **the second generation correlates cannot be implemented successfully unless the first generation correlate standards are present in the school.** In one sense, the second generation correlates represent a developmental step beyond the first and, when successfully accomplished, will move the school even closer to the mission of **Learning for All**.

① Safe and Orderly Environment

The First Generation: In the effective school, there is an orderly, purposeful, businesslike atmosphere which is free from the threat of physical harm. The school climate is not oppressive and is conducive to teaching and learning.

The Second Generation: In the first generation, the safe and orderly environment correlate was defined in terms of the absence of undesirable student behavior (e.g., students fighting). In the second generation, the concept of a school environment conducive to **Learning for All** must move beyond the elimination of undesirable behavior. The second generation will place increased emphasis on the presence of certain desirable behaviors (e.g., cooperative team learning). These second generation schools will be places where students actually help one another.

Moving beyond simply the elimination of undesirable behavior will represent a significant challenge for many schools. For example, it is unlikely that a school's faculty could successfully teach its students to work together unless the adults in the school model collaborative behaviors in their own professional working relationships. Since schools as workplaces are characterized by their isolation,

71

creating more collaborative/cooperative environments for both the adults and students will require substantial commitment and change in most schools.

First, teachers must learn the "technologies" of teamwork. Second, the school will have to create the "opportunity structures" for collaboration. Finally, the staff will have to nurture the belief that collaboration, which often requires more time initially, will assist the schools to be more effective and satisfying in the long run.

But schools will not be able to get students to work together cooperatively unless they have been taught to respect human diversity and appreciate democratic values. These student learnings will require a major and sustained commitment to multicultural education. Students and the adults who teach them will need to come to terms with the fact that the United States is no longer a nation *with* minorities. We are now a nation *of* minorities. This new reality is currently being resisted by many of our community and parent advocacy groups, as well as by some educators.

(2) Climate of High Expectations for Success

The First Generation: In the effective school, there is a climate of expectation in which the staff believes and demonstrates that all students can attain mastery of the essential school skills, and the staff also believes that it has the capability to help all students achieve that mastery.

The Second Generation: In the second generation, the emphasis placed on high expectations for success will be broadened significantly. In the first generation, expectations were described in terms of attitudes and beliefs that suggested how the teacher should behave in the teaching-learning situation. Those descriptions sought to tell teachers how they should initially deliver the lesson. High expectations meant, for example, that the teacher should evenly distribute questions asked among all students and should provide each student with an equal opportunity to participate in the learning process.

Unfortunately, this "equalization of opportunity," though beneficial, proved to be insufficient to assure mastery for many learners. Teachers found themselves in the difficult position of having had high expectations and having acted upon them—yet some students still did not learn.

In the second generation, the teachers will anticipate this and they will develop a broader array of responses. For example, teachers will implement additional strategies, such as reteaching and regrouping, to assure that all students do achieve mastery. Implementing this expanded concept of high expectations will require the school, as an organization, to reflect high expectations. Most of the useful strategies will require the cooperation of the school as a whole; teachers cannot implement most of these strategies working alone in isolated classrooms.

High expectations for success will be judged, not only by the initial staff beliefs and behaviors, but also by the organization's response when some students do not learn. For example, if the teacher plans a lesson, delivers that lesson, assesses learning and finds that some students did not learn, and still goes on to the next lesson, then that teacher didn't expect the students to learn in the first place. If the school condones that teacher's behavior through silence, it apparently does not expect the students to learn, or the teacher to teach these students.

Several changes are called for in order to implement this expanded concept of high expectations successfully. First, teachers will have to come to recognize that high expectations for student success must be "launched" from a platform of teachers having high expectations for self. Then the school organization will have to be restructured to assure that teachers have access to more "tools" to help them achieve successful **Learning for All**. Third, schools, as cultural organizations, must be transformed from institutions designed for instruction to institutions designed to assure learning.

③ Instructional Leadership

The First Generation: In the effective school, the principal acts as an instructional leader, and effectively and persistently communicates the mission to staff, parents, and students. The principal understands and applies the characteristics of instructional effectiveness in the management of the instructional program.

The Second Generation: In the first generation, the standards for instructional leadership focused primarily on the principal and the administrative staff of the school.

In the second generation, instructional leadership will remain important; however, the concept will be broadened and leadership will be viewed as a dispersed concept that includes all adults, especially the teachers.

This is in keeping with the teacher empowerment concept; it recognizes that a principal cannot be the only leader in a complex organization like a school. With the democratization of organizations, especially schools, the leadership function becomes one of creating a "community of shared values." The mission will remain critical because it will serve to give the community of shared values a shared sense of "magnetic north," an identification of what this school community cares most about.

The role of the principal will be changed to that of a leader of leaders, rather than a leader of followers. Specifically, the principal will have to develop his/her skills as coach, partner, and cheerleader. The broader concept of leadership recognizes what teachers have known for a long time and what good schools have capitalized on since the beginning of time—namely, expertise is generally distributed among many, not concentrated in a single person.

(4) Clear and Focused Mission

The First Generation: In the effective school, there is a clearly articulated school mission through which the staff shares an understanding of and commitment to instructional goals, priorities, assessment procedures, and accountability. Staff accepts responsibility for students' learning of the school's essential curricular goals.

The Second Generation: In the first generation, the effective school mission emphasized teaching for **Learning for All**. Did this really mean all students or just those with whom the schools had a history of reasonable success?

When it became clear that this mission was inclusive of all students, especially the children of the poor, another issue surfaced. It centered itself around the question: Learn what? Partially because of the accountability movement and partially because of the belief that disadvantaged students could not learn higher-level curricula, the focus was on mastery of mostly low-level skills.

In the second generation, the focus will shift toward a more appropriate balance between higher-level learning and those more basic skills that are truly prerequisite to their mastery. Designing and delivering a curriculum that responds to the demands of accountability, and is responsive to the need for higher levels of learning, will require substantial staff development.

Teachers will have to be better trained to develop curricula and lessons with the end in mind. They will have to know and be comfortable with the concept of backward mapping, and they will need to know task analysis. These tools of the trade are essential for an efficient and effective results-oriented school that successfully serves all students.

Finally, a subtle, but significant, change in the concept of school mission deserves notice. Throughout the first generation, effective schools proponents advocated the mission of teaching for **Learning for All**.

In the second generation, the advocated mission will be **Learning for All**. The rationale for this change is that the "teaching for" portion of the old statement created ambiguity (although this was unintended) and kept too much of the focus on "teaching" rather than "learning." This allowed people to discount school learnings that were not the result of direct teaching. Finally, the new formulation of **Learning for All** opens the door to the continued learning of the educators, as well as the students.

⑤ Opportunity to Learn and Student Time on Task

The First Generation: In the effective school, teachers allocate a significant amount of classroom time to instruction in the essential skills. For a high percentage of this time, students are engaged in whole class or large group, teacher-directed, planned learning activities.

The Second Generation: In the second generation, time will continue to be a difficult problem for the teacher. In all likelihood, the problems that arise from too much to teach, and not enough time to teach it, will intensify. In the past, when the teachers were oriented toward covering curricular content and more content was added, they knew their response should be to speed up. Now teachers are being asked to stress the mission that assures that the students master the content that is covered. How are they to respond?

In the next generation, teachers will have to become more skilled at interdisciplinary curriculum and they will need to learn how to comfortably practice organized abandonment. They will have to be able to ask the question, "What goes and what stays?"

One of the reasons that many of the mandated approaches to school reform have failed is that, in every case, the local school was asked to do more! One of the characteristics of the most effective schools is their willingness to declare that some things are more important than others; they are willing to abandon some less important content to be able to have enough time dedicated to those areas that are valued the most.

The only alternative to abandonment would be to adjust the available time that students spend in school, so those who need more time to reach mastery would be given it. The necessary time must be provided in a quality program that is not perceived as punitive by those in it, or as excessive by those who will have to fund it.

These conditions will be a real challenge indeed!

If the American dream and the democratic ideal of educating everyone is going to move forward, we must explore several important policies and practices from the past. Regarding the issue of time to learn, for example, if the children of the disadvantaged present a "larger educational task" to the teachers and if it can be demonstrated that this "larger task" will require more time, then our notions of limited compulsory schooling may need to be changed.

The current system of compulsory schooling makes little allowance for the fact that some students need more time to achieve mastery. If we could get the system to be more mastery-based and more humane at the same time, our nation and its students would benefit immensely.

⑥ Frequent Monitoring of Student Progress

The First Generation: In the effective school, student academic progress is measured frequently through a variety of assessment procedures. The results of these assessments are used to improve individual student performance and also to improve the instructional program.

The Second Generation: In the first generation, the correlate was interpreted to mean that the teachers should frequently monitor their students' learning and, where necessary, the teacher should adjust his/her behavior. Several major changes can be anticipated in the second generation.

First, the use of technology will permit teachers to do a better job of monitoring their students' progress. This same technology will allow students to monitor their own learning and, where necessary, adjust their own behavior. The use of computerized practice tests, the ability to get immediate results on homework, and the ability to see correct solutions developed on the screen are a few of the available tools for assuring student learning.

A second major change that will become more apparent in the second generation is already underway. In the area of assessment, the emphasis will continue to shift away from standardized norm-referenced, paper-pencil tests and toward curricular-based, criterion-referenced measures of student mastery.

In the second generation, the monitoring of student learning will emphasize more authentic assessments of curriculum mastery. This generally means that there will be less emphasis on the paper-pencil, multiple-choice tests, and more emphasis on assessments of products of student work, including performances and portfolios.

Teachers will pay much more attention to the alignment that must exist between the intended, taught, and tested curriculum. Two new questions are being stimulated by the reform movement and will dominate much of the professional educators' discourse in the second generation: "What's worth knowing?" and "How will we know when they know it?"

In all likelihood, the answer to the first question will become clear relatively quickly, because we can reach agreement that we want our students to be self-disciplined, socially responsible, and just.

The problem comes with the second question, "How will we know when they know it?" Educators and citizens are going to have to come to terms with that question. The bad news is that it demands our best thinking and will require patience if we are going to reach consensus. The good news is that, once we begin to reach consensus, the schools will be able to deliver significant progress toward these agreed-upon outcomes.

⑦ Home-School Relations

The First Generation: In the effective school, parents understand and support the school's basic mission and are given the opportunity to play an important role in helping the school to achieve this mission.

The Second Generation: During the first generation, the role of parents in the education of their children was always somewhat unclear. Schools often gave "lip service" to having parents more actively involved in the schooling of their children. Unfortunately, when pressed, many educators were willing to admit they really did not know how to deal effectively with increased levels of parent involvement in the schools.

In the second generation, the relationship between parents and the school must be an authentic partnership between the school and home. In the past, when teachers said they wanted more parent involvement, more often than not they were looking for unqualified support from parents. Many teachers believed that parents, if they truly valued education, knew how to get their children to behave in the ways that the school desired.

It is now clear to both teachers and parents that the parent involvement issue is not that simple. Parents are often as perplexed as the teachers about the best way to inspire students to learn what the school teaches.

The best hope for effectively confronting the problem—and not each other—is to build enough trust and communication to realize that both teachers and parents have the same goal—an effective school and home for all children!

References

1. Hutchins, Robert. *The Conflict of Education in a Democratic Society.* Harper, New York, 1953.

2. Gagne, Robert M. *Conditions of Learning.* Holt, Rinehart & Winston, Inc., New York, 1965.

3. Deming, W. Edwards. *The New Econoomics For Industry, Government, and Education.* Massachusetts Institute of Technology, Center for Advanced Engineering Study, Cambridge, MA, 1989.

4. Ibid.

5. Argyris, Chris. *Knowledge for Action: A Guide to Overcoming Barriers to Organizational Change.* Jossey-Bass Inc., San Francisco, CA, 1993.

6. Anderson, Lorin W. and Herbert J. Walberg. *Timepiece: Extending and Enhancing Learning Time.* NASSP, Reston, VA, 1993.

7. Bloom, Benjamin, S. "The Search for Methods of Group Instruction as Effective as One-to-One Instruction," *Educational Leadership*, May 1984, pp. 4–17.

8. Canady, Robert Lynn, and Michael D. Rettig. *Block Scheduling: A Catalyst for Change in High Schools.* Eye on Education, Inc. Princeton, NJ, 1995.

9. U. S. Department of Education, National Center for Education Statistics, National Household Education Survey (NHES), 1993.

10. Sarason, Seymour B. *Letters to a Serious Education President.* Corwin Press, Inc., Sage Publications, Inc., Newbury Park, CA, 1990.

11. Edmonds, Ronald. "Effective Schools for the Urban Poor," *Educational Leadership*, October 1979, pp. 15-18, 20-24.

About the Author

Lawrence W. Lezotte has long been recognized as the preeminent spokesperson for effective schools research and implementation. As a member of the original team of researchers, Dr. Lezotte, together with Ronald Edmonds and Wilbur Brookover, conducted many of the initial studies of effective schools—schools where all students can achieve academic success.

Effective schools describes a school improvement process that is data-based and data-driven, with effectiveness measured in terms of both quality and equity. These criteria assure a high standard of achievement that does not vary significantly across the subsets of a school's student population.

Since receiving his Ph.D. from Michigan State University in 1969, Dr. Lezotte has worked actively with school districts and practitioners around the nation to implement school improvement programs based on the premises of effective schools research.

Dr. Lezotte was a member of the Michigan State University faculty for 18 years. Currently, he is senior vice president of Effective Schools Products, Ltd. in Okemos, Michigan.

As a consultant, writer, and public speaker, Dr. Lezotte continues to touch the lives of thousands of educators and hundreds of thousands of students.